A Tale *of*
Silence

A Tale of Silence

True Story of Jonathan Ned Cole

2nd Edition

Reedited and additional paragraphs added

NED M COLE

CONTENTS

Preface 9

Acknowledgements 11

Part 1: Death 13

Chapter 1 15

Part 2: Life 23

Chapter 2 25

Chapter 3 29

Chapter 4 31

Chapter 5 39

Chapter 6 41

Chapter 7 49

Chapter 8 55

Part 3: Afterlife 57

Chapter 9 59

Jonathan a few years before he died

DEDICATION

This book is dedicated to Benjamin Don Cole, the two years younger brother of Jonathan Ned Cole. Ben is now more than forty years old yet the pain of still not having his brother is a source of never ending agony. When Ben was just a tiny little boy who had not yet learned to walk or talk, Jon taught Ben's little hands to communicate in the language of the deaf. Ben loved his older brown bother with all his heart. Ben like his Father, Ned M Cole cannot, now twenty-one years later, think or talk about Jon without tears welling from their eyes.

PREFACE

A Tale of Silence

This book is a tale about the life of a deaf boy based upon the true-life story of Jonathan Ned Cole as he might have told the story had he not died so tragically at the age of twenty-six years. Parts of the story about his biological mother and father are fiction. Jon only knew their ethnic origins and that one was white, and one was black. Jon's time in the Pittsburgh Children's Home is based upon what his adoptive parents told him. His time in his bio mother's womb is only as Jon might have imagined that time in his life to be. He was just three months old when the Coles, a white couple, brought him into their home and only six months old when formal adoption papers were signed. Biracial adoptions in the early 1960's were uncommon and the adoption of deaf children of mixed race decent by white couples was rare. The story is one of overcoming almost impossible odds, his love for his family and his family's love for him only to have his life and dreams tragically end when he was all too young. Jon was one of five children. Three of his siblings were white Anglo-Saxon children born to Ned and Carol Cole. His fourth sibling was Benjamin Don Cole a boy of American Indian, Italian and Afro-American decent. As Jon looks down on his family from his perch high above the forest, he wished that his Mom and Dad and his two much loved sisters and two brothers would somehow get past the seemingly endless agony of him dying so young. Jon's love for his adoptive family knew no limits. This is not to say that being away from his family to attend schools for the deaf did not cause him many moments of tears. But what sustained him was a certainty that his family loved him with all their hearts. Jon never expressed to his adoptive interest in knowing who his biological parents were. As far as Jon was concerned his "real" mother and father were Carol and Ned Cole. When Jon signed about his adoptive mother and father, he often referred to them as his "Real Mom and Dad". For this reason in the book's narrative reference to his mother and father is capitalized.

ACKNOWLEDGEMENTS

Much of the story of Jon's life is transcribed from the collective memories of him by his adoptive mother, Carol Cole, and his four siblings, Carrie, Regina, Jeff and Benjamin. Many people who knew Jon well, too many to mention, graciously related to the author many sad and humorous memories they held in their minds. As nearly all of them told of their memories of Jon, tears would well into their eyes. The author is deeply indebted to all of them.

PART 1

DEATH

CHAPTER 1

I am Jonathan Ned Cole, a deaf, adopted, brown-skinned son of Ned and Carol Cole. I have been told that I am of German and African American descent. That lineage means not a hoot to me. What has great feeling to me is that I was a dearly loved member of the Cole family. When I was but a little e fellow, I built in my mind a tower so that I could see over the trees. From on top of the trees, I could see a beautiful blue sky and a warming sun. Each day, I watched many happy birds fluttering about. I could not hear them chirp, of course. I was quite deaf. I was not aware at the time, and for sure not concerned, that on the floor of the forest were evil spirits writhing about that would one day bring tragedy to me and dash all my hopes and dreams.

I was born on July 6, 1972, to a white-skinned mother and a dark-skinned father. I guess my biological mother and father were handsome, because folks often told me that I was quite a handsome young man. The ladies seemed to think so.

Sadly, I had to spend most of my days, from when I entered first grade until I graduated from college, away from my family. Decent schools for deaf children never seemed to be close to my home. I knew that having me spend so much time away was difficult for my family, as being away very much was for me. My adoptive parents knew that if I was to ever realize my dreams, I needed a good education. I understood. But that knowledge did not dim the pain of missing my family so many days of my life.

I never knew my bios and cannot say that I ever had a desire to know them. They abandoned me, after all. I must tell you though that my biological mom must have had some good in her, because she very well could have aborted me right off. She did not, so I was given the gift of life.

I for sure was a pretty little child. I know that because I was named the 1976 National Poster Child for the Deaf. I remember the day well. I was presented the award by Franco Harris, the great Steelers running back, in the downtown Pittsburgh office of a social agency for the deaf. I remember that he also gave me a small stuffed giraffe. I loved that gangly little creature. I can still see in my mind's eye my dad standing to the side, in awe of being in the same room as the great Franco Harris.

From birth, I was profoundly deaf. I was told that my bio mom must have contracted measles during her pregnancy. Measles damages nerves between the inner ear and brain. I have the most severe kind of deafness, I am told. Truth be told, I cannot hear a darn thing. I can feel the vibration of a base drum, I can feel the crash of thunder from the top of my head to my toes, and if music is loud enough, I can feel the beat as the sound waves crash into my body. I could never understand why people jumped to the sound of thunder. I loved it. I never heard music (not that I had a clue as to what music really was), the chirping of birds, the rushing of waves, or the cooing of my mother. I must tell you that I regret not hearing the sound of my Mom, Carol Cole. My Mom was a saint and so pretty.

From my vantage above the trees, I often smiled at the sights surrounding me. I did not know and seemed never to imagine that I was doomed. My life ended in a somber retreat from living by a tragic event that need not have happened. I was but twenty-six years old.

Happy that the Christmas event was near those twenty- one years ago, I returned from a Christmas shopping spree to the home of my Mom and Dad, who were visiting friends in Chicago. I was sure that the gifts I so carefully selected would bring joy to my Mom and Dad and to my siblings, Carrie, Regina, Jeff, and Ben, when they opened their surprises on Christmas Day. I loved my family with all my heart. And never a day went by that I did not know in my deepest being that they loved me too.

When I returned home from my Christmas shopping foray in my beautiful red Ford Mustang convertible, I remember being joyously greeted by my dog, Pepper, and my cat, Koko. Pepper stood right inside the garage door, tail wagging, and Koko stood just behind, purring away. I knew that Koko was purring because he rubbed up against my leg in a cat's way of saying, "Hello. Good to see you."

I carried my gifts of love down the long hall leading from our garage to the main part of our house. As I walked to my Mom's office hideaway to wrap my gifts, I could not help but notice the beautiful staircase that wound its way from our ground floor to three upstairs bedrooms and baths. I just loved that stairwell. A few years back, my Dad had commissioned an artist to paint a beautiful Roman-type mural all the way to the top. He honored me by having the artist paint a small figure of me walking along a distant beach.

I was on my way to our spare room, where I was sure I would find a stash of festive Christmas wrappings kept there by my Mom.

After wrapping my gifts, I lumbered back to the garage to press the garage door down button. I could see my Mom signing to me, "Jon, close the door."

Back I ambled to our kitchen. *Ambled* is the right word for it. I had been partly paralyzed on my right side from a serious automobile accident three years earlier. Walking was a chore for me. As I watched the large outside garage door close, I wondered why other people often startled with the first clank of a closing garage door. But I was deaf, you know. What was there to hear of a garage door closing? The soft sound of my red Ford Mustang's motor running blended with the noise of the door closing. But I heard none of this. I only saw. There is nothing to see of a running automobile engine.

With my Christmas packages deposited under our brightly lit Christmas tree, my thoughts turned to the rumblings of hunger in my stomach. You feel hunger. Hearing is not important. Pepper and Koko looked with expectant eyes. They heard the hunger rumblings from my stomach. With a kind stroke of Pepper's head and a gentle pull on Koko's tail, I lumbered with my cane to the pantry, where my Mom kept a seemingly endless supply of Mighty Dog and Fancy Feast. I laughed the sound that only deaf people can make as Pepper and Koko eagerly watched as I dished out their food into separate bowls. Pepper and Koko waited patiently, for they knew that I, once a strapping six-foot athlete of a man, had only my left hand to scoop out the food. My right hand remained curled and limp at my chest, where it had been since that fateful drive on the road from Albuquerque to Roswell that took away forever my skiing and skateboarding joys.

I loved boiled Oscar Meyer hot dogs—bun only. Please, no condiments. I smiled as I remembered my Mom. She, I knew, was the one who magically kept a supply of Oscar Meyers always on hand. While the water boiled, I watched with amusement as the Dr. Pepper fizzled up the side of my glass. Life was a joy with so many things to see from the top of the forest.

The red Ford Mustang purred softly as it spit out its deadly invisible stream.

With a click, our big-screen TV kicked on. Ah, the joys of captioned television. A Dr. Pepper in hand, a nibble on an Oscar Meyer, a vibrating cat (cats vibrate when they purr, you know), a soft, curling, little, old dog, and *The Jetsons* for a laugh—what a joy life was! Soon, Mom and Dad would be home. Soon, Carrie, Regina, Jeff, and Ben would come from far away. My gifts were sure to make my family so happy. Christmas was near.

The red Ford Mustang continued its deadly chore. The Mustang screamed out in silence, "But for a small digital chip to automatically shut me down, I would not do this! Jon loves me! I was Jon's gift from his Mom and Dad for graduating from college. Please! I beg you!"

The picture on the television began to fade away. *Please, dear God, do not take away my sight too. Pepper wake-up. Koko, why have you fallen to the floor? My car! Dear God, help me.* I read about the deadly fumes. *Get up, Jon. Oh, Mom will be so angry with me for knocking Great-Grandpa's picture off the garage hallway wall as I struggle down the long hall to our garage. Help me, dear God. The door. I can see the door to the garage. Must shut off the car. Cannot. The marble floor feels so cold. Help me, Mother.*

Death of one so much loved is a long-lasting agony for those still living who can never again see your smile or watch the look in your eyes as you return their love.

The day I died, my Mom and Dad were at the Chicago O'Hare International Airport when my brother Jeff found them at the US Air lounge. When I died, the cleaning lady who found me in our house frantically called 911 and contacted my sister Carrie in an attempt to find my Mom and Dad. Carrie traced Mom and Dad to the Chicago airport. She frantically contacted Jeff, who lived in the Chicago area. Jeff found Mom in the US Air lounge, waiting for a flight home. Dad was engaged in a meeting with business associates in a conference room nearby. Mom sat quietly reading in the lounge area.

Jeff approached my Mom with a look of anguish on his face. By the look on his face, my Mom knew that something was terribly wrong. In a choked voice, Jeff told my Mom that I had died in our beautiful Port St. Lucie home. Mom screamed in anguish. Then Jeff had the difficult task of telling my Dad. The look of anguish on my Dad's face was heartrending. My Dad rushed to the US Air counter, where he held out his tickets like a child, and with tears streaming down his face, he told the agent that his son had died. He explained to the US Air agent in barely choked-out words that he and his wife needed to go home. The US Air agent immediately arranged for seats on the next American Airlines flight.

As soon as Mom and Dad arrived in Florida, they began the painful task of making funeral arrangements. My Mom looked in the garage at my beautiful red Mustang and cried. With anguish in her voice, she told the Mustang, "I hate you." Dad talked to his friend Steve Wishnowski, who had connections to automobile dealers. Steve drove my red Mustang away and sold it. Sadly, Steve died from Parkinson's disease many years later. His wife Ingrid, a lady I dearly loved, died of ALS a month or so before Steve.

My funeral service was an anguishing time for my Mom and Dad and my sisters and brothers. Dad gave a heartrending eulogy at my funeral service in Port St. Lucie. At the end of what Dad had to say, he could barely choke out the words. Tears streamed down his face. Friends of Mom and Dad from around the country came to the service. At the end of Dad's eulogy, many in the gathering of friends were crying along with my Dad.

For friends of my Mom and Dad who lived in their hometown areas of western Pennsylvania, Mom and Dad arranged for a second service in an old funeral home in West Sunbury, where Mom had lived as a child and as a teenager. At that funeral service, my Dad could find no words to say. For my Mom who stood silently in shock, the aftermath of my death is to this day a blur.

My old friend Steve Ryno drove from Chicago for my internment in West Sunbury. I was buried at a small church cemetery near my Mom's childhood home. When my Mom and Dad pass on, they will be buried next to me. On regular occasions when Mom and Dad are in the area, they stop by my grave to say hello and place lovely flowers at the front of my tombstone.

For nearly a year after I died, my Mom and Dad struggled every day to deal with their grief. For Christmas the year that I died, my Dad purchased a small, under-the-counter television for my Mom. As soon as Dad installed the television, my Mom turned it on and screamed, "I do not want it! It is not captioned!" Irrational, I know. I was not around to enjoy captioned television. Dad and Carrie returned the television to the store where Dad had bought it. Less than one half mile from our house, Dad pulled off to the side of the road where he told Carrie he could not drive any farther.

For several months after I died, my Dad could not sleep. He would get up in the middle of the night for a solitary walk around Ballantrae Golf Club cart paths. He would look up into the sky and curse at the Big Guy for taking me away. On many nights, my Dad would get up in the middle of the night and ride his motorcycle to the funeral home where my Port St. Lucy service was held. He would sit in the front of the building on his motorcycle, hang his head and cry.

Finally, my Dad began to understand that if he was ever to be able to help his family recover, he first had to survive himself. He kept by his bed a pencil and pad. Each of the many times he awoke in the night, he jotted down his thoughts. Finally, he reduced his thoughts to one word. "Survive."

As he staggered around the golf trails leading away from his home, he concentrated on that one word. When he finally was able to reduce his thoughts to that one word, he began the process of helping his family deal with the great tragedy of my death.

My Mom in her own way found a way to deal with her grief. I think she knew that if she was ever to be able to nurture her other children, she too first needed to come to grips with her grief. For nearly the next whole year, my Mom struggled with her grief. A few months after I died, my Mom had the occasion to talk to her new cleaning lady about my death. (The cleaning lady who had found me dead could not bear to enter our house again.) The new cleaning lady told my Mom that she could talk to the dead and had spoken to Jon. She told Mom that Jon said he was fine and that he would love to give her a hug if only he could. I know this sounds foolish, but my Mom chose to believe the woman. Over time, thinking about what the woman told her helped the hole in her heart to slowly grow smaller.

For years my Mom wrote a Christmas letter about the past year of life for her family. In the year ending in 1998, she could not bring herself to write a word. No Christmas letter went out to Mom's and Dad's friends that year. My Mom ultimately was able to live with her grief. At the end of 1999, she began again to chronicle the lives of her family in her Christmas letter. Yet to this very day, my Mom tells my Dad that my death has left a small hole in her heart that will never completely heal.

Mom and Dad, along with Carrie, Regina, Jeff, and Ben, went on with their lives because they had to. Yet I know that in my Dad's case, he never really was able to heal his heart. For my Dad, I was the psychological anchor that he could always rely on to get him through troubled times. For him, no matter what happened to him, he could always know that in his heart, at least he had done one decent thing in his life by adopting me. I wish I had understood at the time how important I was to my Dad.

Like my Dad, my dear brother Ben could never entirely shake the grief of losing me.

When quietly talking to friends who have also lost a child, Mom, Dad, and their friends understand that only those who have lost a child can truly know the depth of the never- ending grief that infects their very souls. Those encounters most often end in a knowing hug and a quiet tear. Oh Ben, Ben I miss you so. Please do not cry.

PART 2

LIFE

CHAPTER 2

Somewhere in a home for unwed mothers, 1972

I must admit that this part of my story about my biological parents is pure fiction. I did not know my bios at all; truth be told, I never really wanted to know who they were. They abandoned me, after all. The parts about me being placed in the Pittsburgh Children's Home are true. Of course, my time at the home for unwed mothers and my time in my bio mother's womb are from my imagination.

There are tidbits of truth in this part of my story because Mom and Dad Cole knew a little about my bio parents and a little about me beginning life in a home for unwed mothers. But for some reason, I felt a need to create a bio mom and dad of whom I could feel proud. My time at an adoption agency in Pittsburg is true. Here goes the beginning part of my life conjured from my imagination.

My bio mother was a quite pretty nineteen-year-old student with auburn hair and emerald eyes at Carnegie Mellon University, an easy distance from her family home in Shadyside, Pennsylvania. Maria majored in political science. Her dream was to one day enter the diplomatic corps. Her family was from a lengthy line of Irish Catholics. Her mother was a devout Catholic who every day except Sunday mornings attended mass at her Sacred Heart church. The church was almost half a mile from where the Mark O'Reilly family made their home at 362 Lehigh Avenue. Their house was a lovely three-bedroom clapboard with fine restaurants and shops walking distance away. Shadyside is a quaint little neighborhood on the east end of Pittsburgh. Its streets are lined with grand old maple and oak trees.

Maria's father, Mark, was a chemical engineer at Pittsburgh Plate and Glass. He had an easy commute to PP& G headquartered in downtown Pittsburgh. Every Sunday morning, Maria accompanied her father to Mass. Her mother, who always attended midnight Saturday Mass, stayed at home to prepare their Sunday meal.

My bio father, Lucian Augustus Roberts, was a handsome, brown-skinned young man born to a light-skinned brown mother and father. His father, Augustus Washington Roberts, was a mechanical engineer working for Westinghouse Electric. Lucian was a star third baseman for the University of Pittsburgh, where he was enrolled in a mechanical engineering program following in the footsteps of his father. In the middle of his freshman baseball season, Lucian ruined his left knee sliding into third base. That ended his baseball aspirations. For his sophomore year, he transferred to Carnegie Mellon to continue his education. At a Theta Chi fraternity party just off campus, he met Maria. He was immediately awestruck by her beautiful auburn hair and emerald-green eyes. It was love at first sight. Two months after secretly dating Mark, Maria became pregnant. Mark immediately proposed marriage. Maria joyfully accepted.

After the first month of pregnancy, Maria's mother confronted Maria about her morning sickness. When she told her mother that she was pregnant to Lucian, a brown-skinned man, her mother went into shock and her father flew into a rage. Her father demanded an immediate abortion. When Maria informed her father that she planned to marry Lucian, he angrily shouted at her, "No f—king n—r will ever marry my daughter. No n—r will ever sit on my knee and call me Grandfather."

Her mother, a devote Catholic, would not consider abortion, which she in her soul believed was a mortal sin. Her mother prevailed.

The very next day, Maria was forced to withdraw from college and sent off to the Booth Home for unwed mothers.

About nineteen weeks into my bio mom's pregnancy, I felt my heartbeat. And I felt the thumping of my bio mother's heart as it pumped life-giving blood through her young body. I was not aware that my bio mother had contracted measles early in her pregnancy. Later I learned that measles cause damage to the audio nerve leading from the ear to the brain. I was rendered profoundly deaf.

My fervent wish is that my bio mother and father went on to live happy and successful lives and hold in their hearts little love for the son they had little choice but to give to a family that would love and cherish me.

Back to the real-life part of my story. Three days after I was born, I was shipped off to the Children's Home located at 5 324 Penn Avenue, Pittsburgh, Pennsylvania. The adoption agency was established in 1893 to care for children without a living mother and father or those bio- parents who did not want them. The residential streets surrounding the Children's Home are lined with trees and just across the street is the BFG Café. When I was in the Children's Home it was the original building built in 1893-94. Today standing on the same lot is a beautiful new brink structure. A kindly, but stern older lady was the manager of the facility when I was there. Mrs. Hohosh demand from her staff loving care for all of us little tots. Sadly, the kindly Mrs. Hohosh has pasted on to her reward for a life devoted to helping little people like me.

CHAPTER 3

Pittsburgh, Pennsylvania, 1972

I vividly recall the day that my soon-to-be Mom and Dad came to visit me at the Children's Home. I was three months old. I quite remember the young couple looking through a glass partition where I was lying in my tiny crib. I saw through the glass a smiling, pretty young woman and a young man point at me and declare, "I want that one!" No one told Mrs. Hohosh to whom she was going to place one of her children.

The time that I spent at the children's home was actually quite pleasant. A very lovely nurse, named Suzy, was an older lady. Often, she would pluck me out of my crib and hug me closely to her body while she placed in my eager mouth a bottle of warm baby formula. When I finished with my bottle, Miss Suzy gently rocked me to sleep in her nearby rocking chair after which she carefully laid me in my tiny crib. As the lights dimmed in my nursery, I would slumber into the dreams of a baby boy whose only wish was to one day have a real mom and dad. I have often wondered what happened to Miss Suzy.

Each morning when I awoke, I looked about and saw the other tiny babies with their red and angry faces throwing their arms about and kicking their legs in all directions. I guess they were hungry. I just lay there and smiled. The whole nursery seemed incredibly quiet to me. I did not know at the time that I was deaf. The nursing home staff did not know I was deaf either. They just thought I was a very pleasant little baby. I think I might have been a staff favorite.

I recall a little girl who for more than a month rested in a crib next to mine. She liked to suck her thumb. I preferred my little finger. We often smiled at each other as we wiggled about in our cribs. The staff gave her the name Cathy. I knew this because the staff placed on the side of her crib facing me a small plaque with her name on it. I'm just kidding. Although I was later tested having an IQ of 158. I must confess it was not until I was about seven months old that I started to learn to read. But somehow, I knew her name. The day she was taken away in the arms of a nice young woman was a sad day for me. I hoped that one day I would see her again. I never did.

The next two months were a joy to me. My (I hoped to be) real mom and dad came to visit me two or three times a week. The staff even permitted my soon-to-be Mom to hold me for a few precious moments each time she visited. Dads were not permitted in the nursery. No one ever explained that rule to me.

Just two months after Cathy left, after my Mom and Dad completed what seemed like a mountain of paperwork and submitted to a home study, Mrs. Hohosh called Mom and Dad to tell them to come to the home to pick me up. I was thrilled. I was going to have a real mother and father.

CHAPTER 4

Murrysville, Pennsylvania, 1972–1980

In early October 1973, Mom and Dad drove me from my temporary home for a thirty-mile ride to my new home on Mamont Road on the outskirts of the small community of Murrysville, Pennsylvania. That was the happiest ride of my life.

As my Dad drove our automobile up the steep, sloping driveway to our house, my eyes were filled with excitement as I caught a glimpse of our lovely two-story brick house some thirty feet up a sharp embankment above Mamont Road. The house was situated on a three-acre, heavily forested lot just east from an old couple who had sold Mom and Dad a three acre lot. The house was set on a clawed- out flat strip up a steep bank. In our small backyard, Dad built a metal-pipe swing set. My sisters, brothers and I spent many lazy summer hours playing on that swing set. Later my Dad built a fine treehouse for us kids. We had fun in the tree house, but I do not know that we appreciated it all that much. We had not built it ourselves.

Within two or three weeks after bringing me home, my Mom and Dad began to suspect that I was deaf. When Mrs. Hohosh was informed, she told my Mom that the children's home would take me back. My Mom's response was forceful and final. "Over my dead body."

I clearly remember the very day I was formally adopted by my Mom and Dad. I remember the worry on their faces as they waited the three months from when they carried me to their home from the Children's Home until an adoption court date was scheduled. They were worried that my bio mother would come back to claim me before the adoption was final.

I remember my Mom holding me in her arms as the adoption judge gave my Mom and Dad a stern lecture about the difficulty of raising a brown skinned kid in a white family. My Mom and Dad rolling their eyes because they knew raising a deaf child would be far more difficult than any racial bias that might be directed their way.

The most exciting day I can remember at our Mamont Road home was when Mom and Dad brought Benjamin into our house. I remember my Mom signing to me that Ben was my new brother. I was thrilled. Ben was brown skinned like me and a mix of African American, Italian, and Native American. His light-brown skin and slightly slanted eyes gave his heritage away. I immediately began to teach Ben sign language. I can recall the first word I taught Ben to sign. We were sitting in our bathtub together. Floating with us was a small rubber alligator. I pointed at the alligator and made the sign for the little beast. Ben's little hands made the same sign.

By the time that Ben was three months old, his little hands could entertain me for hours with his chatter. Ben was nearly four months old before he learned to walk and nearly six months before he learned to talk.

I enjoyed teaching Ben many little things. Ben was always a fast learner. I would laugh to myself when I would think about teaching Ben how to escape from our floor crib.

When I was not more than four, my Dad would load four of us kids onto his Honda motorcycle and ride us up and down the country roads surrounding our area. (Ben was too little.) Not long after, my Dad bought us two small Benelli motorcycles and taught us to ride them. At first, I must admit that my older brother, Jeff, and I were afraid to try out the small motorcycles. Ben was not big enough to even try. My two older sisters, Carrie and Regina, were fearless. They soon shamed the two scaredy cats, Jeff and me, into trying out the two small Benelli motorcycles. From then on, my older brother, two sisters, and I spent more time arguing about who got to ride next than riding the bikes.

When I was still quite small, my Dad built a wooden snow sled he would pull behind his Suzuki trail bike. We children spent many Sunday winter afternoons being dragged around snow-covered fields.

I really liked our house on Mamont Road. My older brother, Jeff, and my younger brother, Ben, were bunked in the same room with me. We had one wonderful bunk bed and one single bed. We boys occasionally would argue over who got the top bunk.

All of us children had bicycles. I learned to ride in the flat section just outside our garage door. I remember one day when I lost control of my bike and crashed into our garage door. I was afraid that one of my siblings would tell my Dad. They probably did, but I never remember my Dad saying anything about the dink in his garage door. I guess my Dad remembered some of the shenanigans he got involved in when he was a kid. Sometimes my Dad would tell us kids about times that his dad let him off for incidents a bit more egregious than a small dent in a garage door.

I was enrolled in kindergarten when I was just over four years old. There was no kindergarten for deaf children near our home. My Mom solved the problem by hiring herself out as a taxi driver. For two years, rain, snow, or shine, my Mom drove me and several other kids from our home to a special program for deaf children in Pittsburgh nearly thirty miles away. I remember one particularly scary winter ride to school. Mom slid off the road into a ditch. A wrecker had to drag us back onto the road. The other children were very frightened. I cannot honestly say that I was. I thought the whole incident was a hoot. I had to hide my laughter from my Mom, who did not think the event all that funny. My Mom, bless her heart, became a foster

33

mother to two little deaf girls for a year or so. One was named Angie. The name of the other little girl escapes me. Both of the two little girls, along with some other deaf children, rode to kindergarten every day with Mom and me.

I recall that at first, my grandfather Cole was a bit put off by the fact that my Mom and Dad had brought a brown kid into their all-white family. My grandma Cole was not put off at all. Grandma was furiously defensive when it came to her children. She rarely criticized whatever they did. My Dad later told me that a few weeks after bringing me into what was to become my home, he had a serious conversation with his father. He told his father that he had two choices: He could either accept me as his grandson or have no son.

Grandpa Cole was a man of high principle and integrity. Not long after, Grandpa Cole visited us at our Mamont Road dwelling. He knelt by my floor crib in front of our large family room window. He grasped my little hands with his bony fingers, and with tears in his eyes, he begged me to forgive him. My Dad, unbeknown to his father , was standing just outside the room. Dad witnessed the whole scene. From that time on, my grandpa Cole could not have been kinder or nicer to me. Oftentimes, when my Mom and Dad and we children visited Grandpa and Grandma Cole in Rocky Grove, Pennsylvania, Grandpa would take us to his Church of God located a not many blocks away on Fox Street. Grandpa always proudly introduced me to his church friends as his grandson.

Grandpa seemed to enjoy becoming somewhat of a celebrity in his church.

My Mom's father, James Vensel, was in many ways a principled man but reacted to Mom and Dad bringing a brown kid into their home rather harshly. His only pronouncement on the subject was "No n—r will ever sit on my lap and call me Grandpa." He died with those words on still firmly buried in his mind. My grandma Vensel never outwardly expressed racial bias toward me, but I often sensed tension in her when I was around. Grandma Vensel was, until her death, very loyal to her memory of her "Jimmy."

Usually each summer, Mom and Dad would pack up us kids and take off for a weeklong vacation. The week or ten days we spent in the summer of 1974 at Gallaudet College for the Deaf, located in Washington, DC, was my favorite. What a time I had there! I was immediately surrounded by other deaf children just like me. That I was brown skinned seemed not to matter a wit to these newfound friends. The other deaf children taught me much improved sign language. Fortunately, I was always a superior learner. Until that time, I was taught only by those who were convinced that deaf people could be taught to talk. I do not think that I ever even learned to verbalize the simple word *mom*. What a thrill it was to be able to communicate with people. All day and late into each evening, we would sign with our little fingers until they were numb. Only with great reluctance would we agree to be hustled off to bed.

On several days, the college took us on outings to see the wonderful sites in our nation's capital. The most memorable was our visit to the Lincoln Memorial. I remember standing at the foot of the bigger-than-life statue of Abraham Lincoln sitting in a beautiful throne-like chair. I could only read a few words my Mom had taught me earlier before I started kindergarten. But I knew the beginning words of Lincoln's famous address word for word, because on many evenings, my Dad would read those words to us children. "Four score and seven years ago, our forefathers brought forth on this continent a new nation conceived in liberty and dedicated to the proposition that all men are created equal …" Later when I learned to read much better, I read Lincoln's Second Inaugural Address. The phrase "Malice toward none; charity for all" was my favorite line of that speech. To this day, the words from those two documents reverberate in my mind. Abraham Lincoln was my hero.

One of my favorite things to do with my family was to visit the Pittsburgh Zoo. I was always thrilled to see the many animals. I think that my favorite animals were the monkeys. As I would watch their antics, I would laugh and laugh.

Most of my memories of my life on Mamont Road were good. I can remember only one incident that was not one I take immense joy in thinking about. The porch at the front of our house was raised about two and a half feet above our small front yard. When I was three years old, I foolishly jumped off the front porch and landed on the instep of my foot. Crack. I spent the next few months hobbling around in a cast.

I cannot say that being a black person in a mostly white society bothered me all that much. Only on occasion did I let myself feel sorry for myself for being different. Many racially biased incidents occurred, but I did not spend much time dwelling upon them.

On occasion we would visit my Mom and Dad's good friend, Sally, Ferguson, who lived in a nice apartment in Shadyside, a section of Pittsburgh. "Aunt Sally" as I named her was a flower child of the sixties and remains one to this day. She acted in wacky ways at times. But I loved her. She was very kind to me. Sally adopted a brown skinned little girl. We became good friends. On a sunny afternoon, Sally's adopted son, Nathan, and I were riding our bikes on the village's shady streets when a nasty white man happened by. He shouted at me, "You dirty n—r, get off my street!" Of course, I did not hear a word of his bigotry. When we returned to Sally's house, Nathan told about it to my Mom and Sally. I could see by the anger on their faces that Nathan had told them something that was very disturbing to them. When I asked what they were talking about, Mom just told me that Nathan told them about a man who shouted at me. Only later did I learn from Ben what the white man actually said. Even then I cannot say that I became angry with the white man. I hoped that I would meet him some day and become his friend. Sadly, I never saw the man again.

I remember another incident that happened when Ben and I were little enough to ride in a grocery cart. As my Mom pushed us down an aisle, a white woman stopped us and said in a snarky voice with her hands on her hips, "What are you going to do with *those* children?" My Mom replied in a calm voice, "I am going to raise them." My Mom was great that way. The arrows that were often directed toward her when she shopped in stores in a few miles from our house with Ben and me did not seem to cause anything but a calm reaction in her.

Mom and Dad had met in 1960 at Slippery Rock State Teachers College, where they were students. In 1961, they slipped away to Cumberland, Maryland, to be married. In January my Dad graduated. He was able to secure a teaching position in the little upstate town of Addison, New York. Mom, the always faithful wife, took a sabbatical from college to be with my Dad. In the late summer of 1962, Dad enlisted in the United States Air Force. Mom followed Dad around the country. After a little over five years on active duty, Dad resigned his commission and made his way back to Pennsylvania.

After a few short years, Mom was able to return to finish her bachelor's degree in English when she enrolled in Chatham, a women's college on Woodland Avenue in study of deaf Pittsburgh. Mom chose for her senior elective to conduct a study of deaf education in Pennsylvania. For source material, she managed to secure a student study program at the Western Pennsylvania School for the Deaf. The school was unaware that Mom was the mother of a deaf child. The final report she issued was devastating. In the meantime, Mom and Dad had become friends with Lee Taddonio. Lee ran for state assembly and won partly due to campaign help from Mom and Dad. Mom and Dad sought Lee's help in improving deaf education in Pennsylvania. Lee was helpful in bringing about changes in state laws that regulated schools like the Western Pennsylvania School for the Deaf. To put additional pressure on the school, Mom and Dad formed an advocate association for parents of deaf children to lobby for changes in deaf education. The results of Lee's and Mom's and Dad's efforts were dramatic. Thanks to Lee, Mom, Dad, and the many parents of deaf children, many improvements were made in deaf education. No longer did schools insist on the hopeless task of trying to make talking people out of deaf children. Instead, sign language became the language of choice for deaf educators. Finally, deaf education moved beyond the Helen Keller syndrome. Unfortunately for me, the changes did not come about until I was well into middle school. By then, my family had moved to Denville, New Jersey. In less than two years later, we moved to Glenview, Illinois. Ultimately in 1993, my family made Placitas, New Mexico, home. I trailed along with them.

CHAPTER 5

Denville, New Jersey, 1980–1982

I remember our house in Denville as a nice, two-story colonial on a pleasant suburban street. All five of us Cole children moved into that house, along with Mom and Dad. Regina, Jeff, Ben, and I had upstairs bedrooms. Carrie bunked in our basement bedroom. At night Ben and my older siblings would complain that squirrels running around in our attic kept them awake half the night. I, of course, did not hear a thing so slept soundly through all the commotion. I was lucky that way. I could always fall into a deep sleep within minutes after my head hit the pillow. Ben once told me that he was jealous of my ability to go to sleep so quickly.

In our backyard, we had a partly above-ground, partly below ground swimming pool. My Dad built a solar heater out of black-painted plywood with a clear plastic cover to which he connected our pool pump. Steaming hot water would pour into our pool. Our pool was the most popular place in our neighborhood for kids to hang out.

We lived in Denville a year and a half or so before our family packed up and moved to Glenview, Illinois. Carrie elected to remain in New Jersey. I missed Carrie. She was, aside from Ben and perhaps Mom, the best sign language signer in our family.

Early on, I became quite interested in reading a book called the Bible. In fact, I kept hidden away in my room five different versions. Later on, when I gained access to the Internet, I discovered a website that had a lively, ongoing discussion of the meaning of the Bible's words. I enjoyed considering the five different writings of the Bible. I could never quite make up my mind which version was the most accurate.

My Mom and Dad, I believe, had strongly held beliefs about life's meaning and purpose, but I do not remember them talking a great deal about religion. They did take us to church on regular occasions when we were little. Mostly though, I remember my Dad reading to us children words from the Gettysburg Address, the Declaration of Independence, and the US Constitution. I think that those documents were my Dad's religion. Exactly why I became so interested in the Bible, I am not sure. I just was. Perhaps in part it was because my Dad once told me of the words of a song he learned as a little kid. "Red and yellow, black and white, Jesus loves the little children of the world." I believe that my Mom and Dad really believed those words.

When I was away at school, my Mom and Dad regularly communicated with me by using a small, in-home teletype machine. I had machines available to me at my schools at both Springfield, Illinois and New Mexico. Often in the evenings, we would type back and forth for more than an hour. Mom and Dad would switch off with each other. They thought I did not notice. But I could always tell which one was on the end of their machine. Mom was a better typist than Dad. She could type faster and rarely made a mistake. Dad—not so much.

CHAPTER 6

Glenview, Illinois, 1982–1993

I remember that in 1982, my family moved from Denville, New Jersey, to Glenview, Illinois. My Mom and Dad packed Jeff, Regina, Ben, and me into our light-blue Pontiac and proceeded to drive west on Interstate 80. When we got to somewhere in eastern Indiana, my Dad pulled our Pontiac to the side of the interstate, where the whole family proceeded to have a celebration because our Blue Bird automobile mileage indicator turned over to 100,000 miles. Mom and Dad broke out a bottle of champagne. They gave each of us kids a small sip.

My Mom and Dad had earlier flown to Chicago to find a house. They found an unusual house located on Lakewood Court in Glenview. Glenview was a suburb about thirty miles north of Chicago, just off the John F. Kennedy Expressway. We were able to move right into our new house. I remember the first look I got of our house. It looked quite odd. The house was clad with diagonal cedar siding and had a prominent, tall turret right in the front. The house was located on a short cul-de-sac just a block away from a small grade school.

Over the eleven years that my family lived in that odd house, Mom and Dad seemed to be in a continuous state of remodeling. All the remodeling was accomplished by a young man named Steve Ryno. Steve had red hair and a red beard. He was rough and tumble in some ways, but at heart, he was a kind, gentle man and a very skilled carpenter. Steve built a wooden deck around three-fourths of our house and a gazebo with a hot tub, installed a gas-fired spa heater, remodeled Mom and Dad's master bedroom, remodeled our kitchen, finished our basement, and laid hardwood floors throughout much of our house. I became quite good friends with Steve. I taught Steve some rudimentary sign language. We had many animated conversations. Steve had an easy demeanor about him. I could tell that he liked me. I certainly liked Steve.

Winter and summer, Dad, Jeff, Ben, and I would crawl into our heated spa and enjoy ourselves for as long as we could stand the heat. The wintertime was especially fun. After steaming away at one hundred degrees, we would crawl out of the spa just dressed in bathing suits and make angels in the snow. Those were fun times. Because of our elevated body heat we felt the cold snow not at all.

I remember a sunny afternoon when I had the one and only fight of my life. Ben and I had walked across East Lake Avenue to a city park where we often played. We met two bigger boys, and one began to make fun of my deafness. Ben flew into a rage. As small as Be. jumped n was, he viciously attacked the taunting boy The nasty boy's friend into the fight and threw Ben to the ground. Then he kicked Ben in the ribs. For one of only a few times in my life, I became truly angry. I grabbed the bigger of the two and caught him right on the jaw with a hard, straight right. He fell to the ground in a daze. The second kid still had fight in his eyes. I never gave him a chance. I grabbed him by the throat with my right hand and left-hooked him in the nose and about his ears. When he fell to the ground a bloody mess, the fight was over. I gently helped a still dazed Ben from the ground and led him home.

I remember another incident when I was twelve or thirteen years old. I was riding my bicycle across East Lake Avenue when I was struck by an automobile. I was not seriously injured, just scratched up a bit. My bike put a small dent and scrape in the driver's automobile.

Just a few days later, my Mom and Dad received a letter from the driver (a lawyer) demanding payment to repair his automobile. Luckily for me, I was accompanied by a friend who witnessed the whole scene. He had told my Mom and Dad that I had been struck in a crosswalk. My Dad wrote a letter to the lawyer advising him of what was witnessed and that he was considering a lawsuit against the lawyer. We never heard from the lawyer again.

I remember many times that our family went to the Six Flags America amusement park with American Hearing Impaired Hockey Association (AHIHA) people. I absolutely loved the many rides at Six Flags. My favorite was the roller coaster.

One summer Mom and Dad also took us kids to Disney World in Orlando, Florida. Seeing Mickey Mouse and Donald Duck was great fun. But, what I liked the most were the rides—the wilder the better. I could spin around all day and barely get even dizzy.

When we were little, Ben and I would spin around in our house until we were silly. Ben, after just a few spins, would fall to the floor. I would laugh at Ben and keep on spinning.

When I was six or seven years old, I got involved in playing hockey with the American Hearing Impaired Hockey Association founded by Irv Tiahnybik and the great hall of fame hockey player Stan Mikita. Each summer, AHIHA would sponsor a weeklong hockey camp for hearing-impaired children like me. Because of Stan's connections with many Blackhawk greats who volunteered to coach us kids, we learned to skate and play hockey by top-of-the game coaches. We were treated to a wonderful week. Ben, who was not hard of hearing, got to tag along. For Ben, hockey became a lifelong passion. He went on to play hockey in high school and college. Ben later became a quite successful hockey coach at the collegiate level.

Do not get me wrong. I was not happy all the time. I remember crying to Ben about not being able to be as good a hockey player as I wanted to be because of my asthma and because I was deaf. I cried sometimes with Ben because we were different. Neither Ben nor I ever let the rest of our family know about our occasional sad feelings. But mostly, I was happy and saw great joy in being alive and being a very much-loved child in my family. To me, family was everything.

I remember many great times at AHIHA. All the deaf kids were fluent in sign language. Most of the staff were fluent also. I had much fun joking and laughing with the other deaf kids and staff. Often, I would stay up late at night in our hotel with all of us deaf kids telling our experiences.

Nearly all my experiences at AHIHA were a great deal of fun. But I remember one incident that caused me to feel terrible. I was skating around the ice when Father Murphy tripped over me. I felt terrible for hurting the poor old man. I left the ice and went by myself to the player's locker room. I sat on a bench and cried. I really did not like to hurt people. A kind staff member came into the locker room and noticed that I was crying. She signed to me "What is wrong, Jon?" I signed to her what happened. I signed to her that I did not want to get on the ice again because I did not want to hurt anyone else. She signed to me that it was an accident. She explained that Father Murphy had been skating backward and simply tripped over me. She told me that Father Murphy was fine. I smiled in my way of saying thank-you and got back on the ice. Ben often told me that many people told him that I had an infectious smile. I guess I did, because when I met people, I always smiled. They always smiled back at me. I liked people, and they seemed to like me in return. Liking people and having them show their kindness in return always made me feel good.

When I was attending school at the Southern Illinois School for the Deaf, I played on a local peewee hockey team. I was the only deaf kid on the team. I had the good fortune to have a great coach. Because of my asthma, I could not stay on the ice for long or skate the length of the ice rink more than a time or two. My coach had me hang back by center ice. As soon as one of our players gained control of the puck, he would pass it to me. I was an exceptionally good skater and puck handler. In one of the games, I got a three-goal hat trick. My Mom and Dad were there to see the game. I was so proud.

There were no grade or high schools near our Denville home for the deaf which my Mom and Dad thought were suitable for me, So I was enrolled in the Illinois School for the Deaf in Jacksonville, a suburb of Springfield, Illinois. Springfield was about 250 miles south of Glenview. Although I understood that the southern Illinois school was an educational experience I needed, being away from home for such long stretches of time was sad for me. But I adjusted. At the school, I was surrounded by manyother deaf children. All my teachers were fluent in sign language. My room was small but furnished nicely with some of my own furniture. I quickly made many friends, including boys and girls. I did not dwell on my loneliness but dedicated to learning all that I could. On occasion, my Mom and Dad would drive to Springfield to visit me. Most times, my Mom was the one who drove me to school and picked me up for school holidays. Dad was often out of town for his work. The campus for our school had numerous classrooms and dormitories. A few of the students' parents lived nearby in Springfield so the kids were able to commute to school daily.

The day I graduated high school in 1990 was a day of joy for me. I had the whole summer to be home with my family. I was able to spend days on end with my favorite person in the world, my brother Ben.

In the fall of that year, I was accepted at Rochester Institute of Technology for my freshman year, majoring in computer science. I did not like RIT much. Most of the kids were only interested in partying. The school had what I thought was a really dumb rule. Students were permitted to have "only one" case of beer in their rooms. Can you believe it? In New York State, the drinking age was eighteen.

I did have some fun at RIT. One very cold winter day, my roommates decided to take a trip to Lake Erie. They invited me to ride along. When we got to the beach, it was a sunshiny day but quite cold. I could see chunks of ice floating in the lake . My friends decided it was too cold to go into the water. Not me. I loved cold weather and especially loved cold water.

I stripped off my shirt and waded into the water in just my shorts. I always wore shorts—rain, shine or snow. The water felt great. I was quite warm from the automobile ride to the lake. My roommates insisted on running the car heater on high. I stayed in the water for ten minutes or so up to my chest. My friends were amazed. None of them ventured into the water. When I next saw my Mom, I told her about my trip to Lake Erie. She asked me if the water was cold. I signed to her that the water felt great. Mom just laughed.

I hung in there for one year at RIT, after which I transferred to Eastern New Mexico University in Roswell, New Mexico. I liked Eastern NM much better. There were many deaf kids like me. The dry air suited me, and the campus was quite nice. I continued working on a degree in computer science.

One very fond memory, yet a sad one, was in regard to a small poodle I called "my black dog." Her actual name was Suzy. Suzy became quite old. She became deaf like me and blind. I loved her dearly.

One day Suzy just could not hang on any longer. She lay down and died. I remember crying many tears and signing to my Mom, "My black dog, I feel so sad." That was the only time I remember (except perhaps when I was just a baby) crying in front of my Mom. I was relieved that my Dad was not there to see me cry. Actually, on occasion I would see my Dad's eyes well up when he would look at me. I could tell by the look on his face that he loved me very much. I loved him too. I just wished that Dad would have been better at sign language. Had my Dad been more capable of signing, we could have had many conversations enjoyable to me. At least we had teletype.

I must admit that I was a little bit afraid of my Dad. He seemed to be a bit stern with us kids. But I always knew that my Dad loved us kids and only did what he thought best to help us to learn and grow into productive adults.

Christmas was always an incredibly happy time for me. I got to come home from school and spend the whole break with my family. I remember one Christmas that my Mom and Dad bought for me a remote-controlled miniature race car. (They of course told me that it was a gift from Santa Claus. Ha ha! I laughed.) I remember spreading the many parts out on the floor in our great room. In about an hour, I put the race car together. I did not need to look at the schematic. I am not bragging, but I was rather good at spatially visualizing things. I remember making all my siblings jealous because I could solve a Rubik's Cube in minutes.

I had great fun with that remote-controlled miniature race car. I would take it out on the paved road in the front of our house and madly race it up and down the street. I think that that race car was my favorite toy. I always loved fast things.

When I got old enough to drive, Mom and Dad bought me a used car. Ben also had a car. Ben's car was faster than mine, so often I begged Ben to let me drive his car. Mom and Dad would have had a fit if they ever had known how fast Ben and I drove those cars around town. It is a wonder that we never got any speeding tickets.

Ben and I always knew that we were different from the rest of our family, but that was okay. We were proud of who we were but mostly so happy to be part of a loving family.

Ben and I used to laugh a great deal together. I remember one time that Ben and I were sitting in a restaurant when a very pretty black girl happened by. She began to hit on me and ignored Ben. Ben was angry for being ignored and told me later that he was jealous of me for being so handsome. I laughed. But I must tell you that Ben was a ridiculously cute young kid. He had no problem attracting the young ladies. I shall leave it at that.

In late summer 1993, my Mom and Dad sold our house in Glenview and moved all of us remaining children to our newly constructed home in Placitas, New Mexico.

CHAPTER 7

Placitas, New Mexico, 1993–1996

The time that I spent in Placitas was perhaps the happiest time of my life. My Mom and Dad built a beautiful house nestled about halfway between the Sandia Mountains and the floor of the Rio Grande Valley. The little town of Placitas was just thirteen or fourteen miles north of Albuquerque. We lived a mile or so from the small Placitas town center. From the back of our house looking west toward a setting sunset, I could enjoy a beautiful scene. I could see the stark peak of Mount Taylor some eighty miles away and the twinkling lights of Albuquerque to the south. Through the large bay window in the front of our house, I never ceased to be thrilled at the sight of the 11,000-foot Sandia Mountains that appeared to lean over top of me.

The most memorable time I can recall included the wonderful days I spent on the ski slopes atop the Sandia range. I loved the crystal-clear, dry air. The asthma I suffered at low, damp altitudes did not bother me at all up near the sky. What a thrill it was to race down the ski slopes on my snowboard. To feel the rushing air water my eyes and the small scrub trees racing by was pure joy. Often, I would ski from early morning until I reluctantly had to ride the tramway back down the mountain slope as the falling sun began to sink over the western horizon.

When my family first moved from Glenview to Placitas, we already had a small house in Port St. Lucie. My Mom and Dad spent about half of the year in Placitas and the other half in Port St. Lucie. I do not remember much about the first little Port St. Lucie house. I guess I was away at school most of the time. By the time of the move to Placitas, both of my sisters were married and had children. Only Mom, Dad, Jeff, Ben, and I moved to New Mexico.

But like all good times, they passed into my rearview mirror.

In the fall of 1993, I enrolled in the Eastern New Mexico College for Deaf, located 231 miles south of Placitas. I was away from my family again. For my major, I chose computer science mainly because my Dad was a computer scientist and I admired the success he experienced in the field.

The first year or so was a lot of fun. I did not drink or smoke or party. But I did enjoy hanging out with my many friends. I spent a good deal of time hanging around our campus bookstore and was able to make friends with the manager. I volunteered to help out around the store every way that I could. Not many weeks went by before the manager offered me a part-time job. I loved the interaction with deaf students who often frequented the store. I always had an easy smile for each student who came to our campus store to buy books or other sundry items. I cannot recall a single student who came to the store and, in a few minutes, I did not have smiling. I really liked people. I guess it showed.

My Mom bought a new Jeep Wrangler, which she often permitted me to drive the 231 miles to and from school on long weekend breaks. One day during my sophomore year at college when I was driving to school on the lonely two- lane Route 285 heading south from Albuquerque to Roswell, a speeding red car swerved into my lane. I immediately swung to the left and lost control of my vehicle. I spun around, rolled my vehicle over, and crashed into a deep ditch on the left side of the road. The red car sped away, leaving me to die.

Luckily for me, a New Mexico state trooper happened by. Of course, I do not remember the immediate aftermath of the crash events because I suffered a severe head injury for which I was rendered unconscious. But to this day, I can remember the red speeding car that nearly ended my life.

As far as I know, the state police never identified the culprit. Later I was told that I was rushed by ambulance to the Roswell hospital's emergency room, where I was attended to by a physician who had recently completed his residency in the brain injury section of Johns Hopkins Hospital. I was lucky because he knew that the latest treatment for brain injury was not to sedate the brain with drugs but to stimulate it.

He followed treatment protocol for brain injuries to immediately reduce brain swelling by packing ice around my head. He saved my life.

After a few days in the Roswell hospital, I was air transported to the Presbyterian Hospital at 1100 Central Avenue, Albuquerque. The evening I arrived, the doctors told my Mom and Dad that most likely I would not survive until the morning. Events proved otherwise. I did not die that night but spent the next month or so lying helplessly in a coma.

My Mom told me that one day while she was holding my hand, I wiggled my little finger. Eventually when I started to come out of the coma, I was transported to a rehab facility just a mile or so from the hospital. At first, I was placed in a bed equipped with high rails to prevent me from falling to the floor.

For the next month or so, my brain was filled with fog. But I was aware that every day someone from my family came to visit me. As I gradually recovered, I began to restlessly flop about. Fearful that I would fall from the bed, the staff moved me to a seven-foot by seven-foot floor crib. Many nights, one of my family members would lie in the crib with me until I fell asleep. I remember many nights my Dad lay beside me. When he would start to leave, I would beg him in sign language to stay. I was almost asleep when I felt my Dad move and scramble away to the crib opening. I scrambled after him. Just as I reached the gate to the crib, the gate sharply closed. My fingers were crushed. My Dad cried. In short order, an ambulance transported me to a nearby emergency room, where my bruised hand was treated. I was returned to the rehab facility a few hours later.

As I gradually recovered, my Mom and Dad would help me into a wheelchair and wheel me for long walks around the rehab facility. Each day I would beg my Mom and Dad, "Please, Jon go home." I could see the anguish on my Mom's and Dad's faces as they tried to explain to me that I needed to stay in the rehab place a little longer.

Early on in my time at the rehab facility, the managing doctor wanted to sedate me to cause less trouble for the staff. Luckily for me, my oldest sister, Carrie, was involved in brain research at the University of New Mexico and knew that sedating a brain-injured person was the worst of all treatments. She helped me sign a letter to the doctor demanding that I not be given sedatives. Because of my family's ongoing argument over treatment options with the head doctor, and because Mom and Dad could no longer bear the look of pain on my face as I begged them, "Please, Jon go home," Mom and Dad checked me out of the facility. The day that Mom and Dad drove me from the rehab facility to our home in Placitas was a happy day for me. When I was first at home, I had to use a wheelchair to get around. But gradually I recovered to the point that I could hobble around with just a cane.

To aid in my recovery, I was enrolled in an outpatient rehab facility in downtown Albuquerque. Each day my sister Carrie, Mom, or Dad—or all three—would transport me to the rehab facility. To tell the truth, I did not enjoy rehab. Many of the exercises the nurses insisted I undertake were exceedingly difficult for me. I remember one day that the rehab nurse assigned a particularly difficult exercise for me to undertake. The exercise was quite painful. In the middle of the routine, I abruptly stopped and began to laugh. The nurse signed to me, "Jon, why did you stop, and why are you laughing?" I replied, "If I did not laugh, I would cry." I was not kidding.

To tell the truth, much of the year following my automobile accident was lost to me. That time only comes back to me in bits and pieces. Mostly the year was one big blur for me.

In many ways, Carrie helped me a great deal in my recovery ordeal. Carrie was a doctoral student at the University of New Mexico studying the workings of the human brain. She understood a great deal about brain injuries and how to best treat them. I must admit that many times as Carrie pushed me toward recovery, I became quite angry with her. One of the therapies she taught me was to visualize those things that I could no longer do. What I missed the most was snowboarding down steep mountain slopes. Carrie taught me how to close my eyes and visualize myself tearing down steep slopes with trees and bushes flying by and snow swirling about as I raced to the bottom. The virtual reality helped me to visualize in my mind something that I loved a great deal. I shall be ever grateful to Carrie for helping me to overcome my disability and focusing on the wonderful life still ahead of me. Nowadays, people can recreate almost any virtual reality on artificial intelligence machines. Unfortunately for me, such machines were not available at the time so I could only imagine fun realities in my mind.

When I recovered enough, I re-enrolled in my college program. Being back at college was great. My many college friends welcomed me back enthusiastically. The bookstore manager gave me back my part-time job.

I was enormously proud the day I received my associate's degree in computer science. I was ready and—I thought— prepared to continue pursuing my dream of getting a good job and having my own family. By the time I finished my college degree, Mom and Dad had rented their house in Placitas to a building contractor family, built a new house in Port St. Lucie, Florida, and moved there. I happily moved with Mom and Dad.

CHAPTER 8

I loved our house in Port St. Lucie. It was a large, two- story, five-bedroom home backing to a mile-wide expanse of the St. Lucie River. Although I spent most of my time away at college when Mom and Dad lived in Port St. Lucie, what time I did spend there I very much enjoyed. I loved the cool marble floors and the staircase that wound its way past a beautiful mural scene painted all the way from the bottom to the top. I had my own bedroom with a handicap bath. By the time my family moved to Port St. Lucie, I had already become partly invalided as the result of my New Mexico automobile accident.

Shortly after I came home to Port St. Lucie, I began volunteer work at our local library. The older lady who ran the library was kind to me and quite generous with her time. She did not know sign language, but we managed to communicate well enough through small written notes to each other. I loved books. The kind librarian did not complain when I buried my nose in a book to the neglect of my book-sorting duties.

I was of the opinion that volunteer work would look good on my resume.

Because I was deemed handicapped by the government, I was given a monthly stipend as long as I remember. I am not complaining, I hurry to add. I always had coins in my pocket. One of my passions was collecting sports cards. I had stored away a box of several thousand. Some were quite valuable. My favorite was a signed original rookie card of the great Chicago Blackhawks hall of famer Stan Makita. Located in Stuart, Florida, only a few miles from my home, was a sports card dealer. I spent many an hour haggling with the owner over the price of sports cards. Sometimes I bought from him, and sometimes I traded him from my substantial stash. I never accepted his first offer. In most cases, after a few days, I would haggle him down to what I considered a good deal. He did not know sign language, but we managed to get by fine with written notes. He was a fun guy to be around. He always looked up with a smile when I entered his store.

My Dad had a forty-one-foot diesel-powered boat he docked at a community marina slip we could see one hundred yards or so from the back of our house. My Mom, my Dad, and I would ride on Dad's boat sometimes out into the Atlantic. Poor Mom would get seasick if the water was even a little rough. I, on the other hand, never got seasick. The rougher, the better. I loved it. On other occasions, we along with guests sailed a few miles up the St. Lucie River until we we came upon a small dam. The river looked much like a Vietnam river scene winding its way north. Along the way, my Mom would point out interesting sights. My favorite was a dilapidated bridge and ramp that were prominently featured in an early James Bond movie.

My Dad bought a Seadoo wave runner, which we kept docked on the St. Lucie River just behind of our house. I loved to race up and down the river, which flowed eight miles out to the Atlantic Ocean. I would spend hours spinning in circles, crashing over the wake of passing power boats, and racing up and down the river at top speed. I just loved it. I guess of all the experiences of living on the earth, one I very much miss is riding a Seadoo. Crippled as I was, I could manage the Seadoo just fine.

As fate would have it, the great joy of being home with my family slipped away just a few days before Christmas 1998.

PART 3

AFTERLIFE

CHAPTER 9

A nice place in the sky, December 1998– 2019

I must tell you that my perch in the sky is quite pleasant. The Big Guy gave me a hammock from which I could sway about and check in from time to time on how my earthly family was doing. I watched with sadness as my Mom and Dad and sisters and brothers slowly recovered from their grief of me passing on to this lovely place. I am especially saddened to know that my Dad and my dear brother, Ben, to this day carry their grief just below the surface. My Mom seems to be coping better.

The most enjoyable part of being here is that I get to chat with some remarkable folks. One of the most interesting is John the Baptist. John is a scrabble-haired, bearded old guy dressed in scrubby clothing. John led a remarkable life on earth. John never took himself all that seriously and had a great sense of humor. He is really a funny guy. He had many stories to tell. I taught John to sign, so he and I have had quite a few animated stories to tell each other. I would tell him about my life on earth, and he would tell me of knowing the Big Guy's son, Jesus, and of his early life when he was somewhat of a disreputable character. He told me with tears in his eyes of how he watched Jesus being crucified on a cross between two criminals. He told me of hearing the words of agony that Jesus spoke just before he died. John sheepishly told me he was the ghost writer for the part of the Big Book that told his story. Many times John encouraged me to author my story. I put him off at the time by telling him I had other things on my mind.

The Big Guy admonished me to not spend so much time getting involved with the folks still living on the earth, but I could not help myself from dropping in on conversations about me between my Dad and Ben. I smiled as Ben would tell my Dad about the wonderful times he and I had spent together. I was pleased when Ben told my Dad that he thought of me as a gentle giant. I was only about six feet, one inch tall, but I guess most folks saw me as a big fellow. Ben was only about five feet, eight inches tall. Ben told my Dad that he never knew anyone who knew me who did not love me dearly. Knowing that now brings warmth to my heart. One day, Ben told Dad that when he told his friends that I had died, they would hang their heads and cry. Ben told Dad that even to this day when he brings me to mind while talking to his old friends who knew me well, tears spring to their eyes. I wish that they knew that I was in a good place now.

One of the first lectures I attended in my big place in the sky was one Moses gave on the burning bush. (Moses always had a sign language interpreter standing by). I have to admit that I was a bit skeptical. But who am I to question the Big Guy's favorite resident? After all, right on the entrance gate to our place in the sky the Big Guy hang Moses's two stone tablets containing the Ten Commandments.

I told my friend John the Baptist one day that I would like to meet presidents George Washington and Abraham Lincoln. John told me that many people also wanted to meet the two giant men of American history. He told me that there was a long waiting list. I asked John to place my name on the list. He agreed to do just that.

Several months later, I was lying in my hammock when a carrier pigeon landed on my stomach. Around the little pigeon's neck was a small note carrier. I snatched the note and read that the two presidents invited me to meet them in three days at precisely three o'clock at their mountain retreat. The note suggested that I may wish to bring a sign language interpreter along. I immediately responded to their

RSVP, replaced the note in the little carrier around the pigeon's neck, and sent the pigeon on its way. I asked my friend John to accompany me. He agreed.

On the appointed day, John and I climbed up the long, winding path to the presidential retreat. The two presidents were sitting in rocking chairs under a large oak tree. Placed in front of the two presidents was a third rocking chair. They bade me to have a seat. President Washington began our conversation with "Son, what do you have on your mind?"

John interpreted, and I responded, "Sir, I am troubled by your position on slavery. Can you tell me why you never freed your slaves?"

President Washington told me that not freeing his slaves was one of his great regrets. He told me that he long believed that slavery and the idea of America that all men are created equal could not long stand if America was to become the embodiment of the ideas expressed in the Declaration of Independence written by Thomas Jefferson. He informed me that because of Virginia law, he could not free his slaves so long as he was in debt. He told me that he was deeply in debt and remained so at his death. President Washington told me that he was deeply saddened that to end slavery in America Americans had to suffer a tragic Civil War. I told President Washington those parts of his story were never taught to me by my history teachers. I thanked President Washington for his reply.

I then turned my attention to President Lincoln.

I asked President Lincoln why he had only freed the slaves held in Confederate states when he issued his Emancipation Proclamation. He told me that his number one motive was to preserve the Union. He told me that although he long believed that slavery was an institution which was a travesty of human behavior, he could not free salves the slave states of Kentucky and Maryland because he feared that such action would cause those two states to secede from the Union. If the Union was not preserved, America would never become the great nation it was destined to be.

I then asked President Lincoln what he thought of General Robert E. Lee, given his Second Inaugural Address in which he stated the words "malice toward none." President Lincoln told me that he believed that if ever the great tragedy of the Civil War was to be healed, the people of the South needed to be welcomed back into the Union and treated with kindness. He told me that although he did not agree with Robert E. Lee's position, he understood why General Lee could not raise his sword against his beloved fellow Virginians.

John signaled to me that my interview with the two presidents was over. I rose from my rocking chair, reached out my hand to President Washington, and thanked him for taking his time to talk to me. He grasped my black hand in his white one and smiled at me. I thanked President Lincoln, and he too grasped my hand as he said, "God bless you, Jon."

John and I then made our way back down the long, winding path toward my hammock.

One day, I had the fascinating occasion to chat with the lady who had written the first chapter of the Big Book. John of course went along to translate. She told me about the so- called bang theory postulated by earthlings. What was really fascinating were her comments on the many places in the vast universe where the Big Guy created life. She told me that the Big Guy pretty much left those planetary beings evolve at their own pace and in their own direction. Surprising to me, the lady told me that in the case of the earth, the Big Guy took a special interest—enough so that he sent his Son to help the earth folks sort out their troubles. She said that the Son was saddened that his efforts met with only partial success. I have not had the occasion to meet the Son. One of these days when I can find the time to look up the Son, I will. He seems like a really nice fellow.

A few weeks later after attending Moses's lecture, I requested an audience with the Big Guy. We met under a shade tree. The Big Guy asked what I had on my mind. I signed to him that I had seen hearing angels sign about something called music and the great joy they experienced listening to great classical music by Tchaikovsky and Beethoven. The Big Guy leaned down to me and placed his hand gently on my head. He whispered in my ear, "Jon, now you can hear."

I immediately began to hear the wonderful sounds of the Fifth Symphony.

I spent the whole rest of the day listening to Beethoven's and Tchaikovsky's many beautiful compositions. I must have watched and listened to the wonderful movie *The Sound of Music* at least a half dozen times. I remembered people signing about the many beautiful gospel hymns sung by a fellow named Elvis Presley.

A few days later, I happened upon Elvis. We had a quite interesting conversation. He told me that he was quite surprised that the Big Guy let him in. He told me that the Big Guy told him he really enjoyed listening to him singing such beautiful hymns. Not so much his other shenanigans.

Often Elvis would put on concerts for the hearing folks who lived with us in the sky. I never went to any of the concerts. I did not get what all the hoopla was about. I told Elvis I had been deaf, but the Big Guy gave me hearing. Elvis immediately reached into his pocket and gave me a front row, center ticket for his next concert. I sat right next to the Big Guy.

For our heaven holiday, John gave me a Blue-Ray player. I traded all my Kindle books and most of my hardcover and paperback books for classical music and Elvis DVDs. I kept my five versions of the Bible and my favorite book, *Jonathan Livingston Seagull*.

Richard Bach's book was a great inspiration to me. Jonathan Seagull's idea that one should strive to do one's utmost best I took to heart. Jonathan Seagull's passion was flying. My passion was sliding ever faster down the slopes of the Sandia Mountains and the steep ski slopes of Taos on my snowboard.

For a time after my automobile accident, I had to give up my passion. I was very depressed. Thanks to my sister Carrie, who taught me to visualize myself flying down the slopes of Taos, I was able to feel again the rush of the wind, the thrill of trees flying by, and passing other skiers on my mad dash to the bottom. But mostly I loved Jonathan Seagull's idea of being kind to people and letting love for people fill my heart. I found that feeling love for others gave me the greatest joy. When I showed love and kindness to others, they returned the love and kindness to me. They accepted me even though I was deaf and black. I felt a need all my life to be accepted. I knew that I was different. I was afraid that because I was different, other people would not like me and be kind to me. I learned that my difference from them was of no concern to them. My Mom and Dad loved me for just being me. From them I learned that I was okay just as I was. The warm hand of love I felt from my Mom and Dad and my brothers and sisters were of great comfort to me.

A few weeks later, Elvis dropped by my hammock. To my surprise, he told me that he would like me to join his band. When he saw the doubt in my eyes, he told me that he would teach me how to play a guitar. In the weeks that followed, almost every day Elvis would stop by my hammock to give me lessons. When he thought I was ready, he asked me to his concert and invited me to his stage. He introduced me as the newest member of his band. Every week or so, I would play my new electric guitar with the band. On off weekends when the Big Guy was out of town, we performed a little rock and roll for the younger crowd.

My friend John the Baptist and I had many discussions on the meaning of the various clauses of the United States Constitution and amendments thereof. From John, I learned a great deal about the evolution of civil rights in the land of my birth. Fascinating stuff for sure. John's explanation of how the Electoral College clause prevents a few big population states from dominating US presidential elections was not a subject I remember ever being presented in my many years of education. I wore out my head thinking about these subjects.

On a cool evening on July 25 , 2019, I felt a chill go through my body. Something was wrong. I took a quick peek at my earthly family.

I saw my dear aunt Snooky crying. I knew right away that my uncle Pat, aunt Snooky's husband had died.

I sadly watched the family for the next few days as they gathered around to comfort each other. I was touched and saddened by the eulogy my aunt Snook had asked my Dad to give at Pat's funeral service. I know that Uncle Pat was a good, kind man. He always greeted me with a smile. I just knew that he liked me, and I for sure like him. I am told it takes a couple of days for paperwork to make its way to the Big Guy for signature, but I expect to welcome Uncle Pat at the pearly gates in a day or so. I have already put in a good word for Uncle Pat with the Big Guy. The Big Guy takes personal recommendations very seriously.

Unusual for him, my friend John, with fire in his penetrating eyes and a scowl on his face, reminded me again of his idea that I should get busy writing the story of my life. The next day, I called Elvis and told him that I needed to take a sabbatical from his band to attend to an important matter. Elvis saw the pleading look in my eyes and kindly told me to take the time I needed. In a few days, I got a chance to chat with the Big Guy about John's idea. The Big Guy told me that I would need an Apple computer and printer and said he could arrange a set for me.

A week or so later, the Apple computer and printer showed up. Shipping was a little slow due to an elf work slowdown over some grievance or the other. I sat in front of my new Apple computer and wrote, "I am Jonathan Ned Cole, a deaf, adopted, brown-skinned son of Ned and Carol Cole ..."

www.ingramcontent.com/pod-product-compliance
Lightning Source LLC
Chambersburg PA
CBHW070940120626
46546CB00004B/1500